# Life during the Darkness

Do not stop before your heart beat stops

OLYPRIYA ROY

ISBN: 978-93-5458-536-4

Published in India 2021 by Pencil

*A brand of*
One Point Six Technologies Pvt. Ltd.
123, Building J2, Shram Seva Premises,
Wadala Truck Terminal, Wadala (E)
Mumbai 400037, Maharashtra, INDIA
**E** connect@thepencilapp.com
**W** www.thepencilapp.com

# Author biography

I am currently a student of English at The Heritage College.I completed my schooling from Nava Nalanda High School. I have a deep passion for writing poetries and short stories. In 2019 ,one of my stories has got published in an anthology named 'Beautiful Minds' which received UGC recognition.Before that ,my poem got published in a magazine named 'Bodhon'.From an early age I was attached in the field of literature.I had a dream of writing my own book and this is my first venture of writing a full book on my own while sitting within a house-arrested condition because of this pandemic.I want to write much more to reach to all ages of readers and give them plesure through the magic of my pen and brain.

# CONTENTS

# INTRODUCTION

The silence and the somber tone that darkness has within it make us find a new light. For the past one year we all have been going through darkness where we are constantly haunted by the fear of death and losing our beloved ones due to the severe outbreak of the pandemic. And it is at this time when I planned of writing the book to express that how I have been constantly in a search of a new light within darkness to combat with this situation. The pandemic has definitely impacted every one of us and has given us quite a tough time but there is always something which can save us from getting devoured by severe boredom and despair. Just we need to find them out .Well we created a silly joke to describe the condition of the students like us at this situation that is "untimely retirement."But in spite of so much negativity around, the pandemic has made us realize once again in a new light "to live and remain happy just with ourselves and our own company." Those happy moments of togetherness with our families and dearest ones, those unmasked laughter, those crazy photo sessions which we never even imagined of giving the slightest importance, have suddenly taken the role as "medicine of our pain". This sudden blow of pandemic has made us accept and realize one truth that every moment is valuable because they gift you with some memories. And memories are more precious than time, because as time it changes everything rapidly but memories remain unchanged and unfaded.

To me Literature has played a very important role in helping me forget all these worldly troubles and agitations around. The literature that came my way during these times are mostly very thought-provoking in nature and acted like therapeutic drugs. Before also I had been through difficult situations where literature provided me solace, but this pandemic has taught me once again the profound influence of literature during hard times. Being a student of English, I have always learnt from my professors the power of literature during the toughest times. That's why there are several ground-breaking literary pieces which have been created during some of the most toughest and tumultuous times in the history of the world. As said by Oscar Wilde "Literature always anticipates life. It does not copy it, but moulds it to its purpose." While reading multiple literary works during these confined days, I gradually started realizing the underlying meaning of the power of literature.

Another thing with which I have developed a strong bond with is nature. My love for nature and natural creatures developed first when I was a little kid like all other kids, I also used to listen to those fairy tales and fables from my mother and from that time, being a highly imaginative kid, I used to dream about those trees and birds which could able to talk and gossip with each other just like we human beings do. Though I have always remained preoccupied with the urban backgrounds, but my flat where I have been staying since childhood has a huge area beyond our balcony covered absolutely with greens. This vast area of greeneries plays a huge influence behind my deep love and awareness for nature. Also it's this place which has invoked my intense love for natural creatures as they seem to be my only mates when I stay in my house. The chirpings of the birds and the cooing of doves act like my alarm in the morning. But in these pandemic days when there is no companion, nature is fully accompanying me in bringing a breath of freshness in my mind and soul. In most of the evenings, a couple of doves and jungle babblers come and sit on the flower tubs placed on the window of my room. I laugh sometimes while seeing the relentless foolish quarrelling of the jungle babblers among themselves just on the point that who is going to sit on which flower tubs. These little mundane things which often remained unnoticed to my eyes suddenly carved out an important place in my mind giving me the ultimate happiness in the bleakest hours also. Nature by herself is a Mother, who has the power to calm and comfort our wretched souls like all our mothers do to their children. Nature is meant to be loved not to be understood always.

Livings simply on the happy memories are indeed hard but that's where my passion for writing this book developed. It's going to be a book that will say the story of pandemic verses us, our struggle, our mental strength to accept all the odds and still standing strong to face the upcoming tempests.

# MISSING THE COLLEGE

"One week, two weeks holiday it was
When we got the news first
But then it turned into a year's holiday
We never knew it was the last day
Of our college that year.
For we thought it was just a separation of two weeks
For then we were ignorant of the upcoming pains
The pain of missing the college life.
Those familiar canteen smells or watching rain with friends were nice
Those familiar lectures of our professors
Their indulgence, loving and laughter together
And all these things we badly miss everyday
For we can find all these not in our present
But just if we go down through my memory lane."

Our love for something reaches at the highest stage when we terribly miss the thing and pining to get it back. To me this statement worked like an infallible truth. My bond with my college reached at the highest level when the college went for a complete shut down due to rapid increase of the covid cases. It was a Saturday evening at around 4 pm when we all heard the news of schools and colleges going into holiday for two weeks. The first reaction I had was that ,I fell a little sad.Because to me my college was not just a place of education but almost my second home. Within a few minutes my whattsapp got flooded with the messages of two weeks holiday. There was a mixed reaction from our classmates. Some were happy for my classmates who stay outside Kolkata could able to go to their homes for two weeks, others were happy with the hope of enjoying an unexpected holiday for continuous two weeks.But none of us thought that day that we would soon start missing the place badly for the two weeks holiday gradually turned into a year's holiday.

I still remember the first day of my journey to The Heritage College.It was in June 2019, my journey with Heritage College began.In the very first day, we had an orientation program. The speaker of the program Sir Clayton Moses uttered one word which I then thought insignificant and it was, "You all will soon start calling this college as your second home. You'll start feeling soon that you have just come from one home to another home." And it happened so indeed. Our college has such a calm and meditative atmosphere that I soon started loving it. Before coming to Heritage, I had one of the toughest times of my life. During the two years of my higher secondary board preparations, I underwent through innumerable nerve-breaking moments and pessimistic days which shattered all my expectations and brought a slight tinge of despair to my mind. For during those two years, I realized the gulf between expectations versus reality. I tried my best to keep myself alienated from those negativities and the constant haunting of the fear of failures in science. I never disliked science and still I like it but it was presented to me in the most wrong way. Science is not a vehicle of competition rather it's a vehicle of giving rise to rational ideas in an individual's mind. And that was the point when I realized the importance and influence of teachers in a student's life. It was then when I realized at the utmost level why getting supportive people in life is so important. I have witnessed failure upon a nearer view during that time. They were some mere academic failures ,but some people around me described the whole situation adding so much colors to it, that it almost brought a pall of darkness upon my parent's and my mind too. But amidst all those pessimism, I learned one thing that was how to keep believe in myself and my capacities. There actually literature provided me the ultimate peace and freedom to my mind. It was then when I started realizing the essence of romantic poetry and how 'melancholia acted as the muse behind the romantic poets creating such masterpieces.' I got attached to literature in a much deeper and deeper way. I extensively started reading some timeless classics of English literature which were mostly poetry. One morning feeling extremely wary of seeing those complicated mathematics problems in my copy, I decided to keep them away and started reading Milton's "Paradise Lost". I never knew how immensely significant this literature piece is in the field of English but I got so engrossed within this magnum opus creation of Milton that I completed reading Book 1 and 2 of Paradise Lost within a few days. I secretly read these books. But I was unaware of one thing that all these depressions of failure had actually worked as a blessing for those failures actually helped me to find the real pleasure and happiness of life through reading literature .Those failures acted as a driving force towards making me get more inclined towards literature and paved my way towards taking up English as my subject in college.

But there's a saying 'After every hardship there is relief.' Likewise after crossing all the hardships of higher secondary exam, I came to Heritage and have found the ultimate joy.During these pandemic ,the college is the biggest thing that I have been missing extremely ,along with the care-free college life,my friends and professors.

# HERITAGE SURFEIT MY EXPECTATIONS

It is a common saying that when you expect nothing from someone or something you get the best from that only.And that's happened to me regarding my college. Before going to Heritage, I had such a tough time that I decided to go to Newcastle University in England for studying English literature there. But suddenly one day my cousin came and he told me, "There's a college called Heritage in Kolkata which has a lovely atmosphere and a beautiful campus." He almost in a way insisted me to have a look at the college through their website. What happened suddenly I don't know my parents in a way forced me to do a registration in this college? I made a very casual registration thinking that it would be useless for I will be flying to Newcastle within two months. These all happened in the month of June. Unexpectedly one afternoon I received a message from Heritage. I remember it was written there, "You have been selected."I was happy but hesitant though for I was preparing to leave for England within a month .But maybe God had some greater plans for me which I then could not realize. Dad suddenly decided to admit me to Heritage the next day. After all the admission process to this college were over, dad told me to wait and see whether I like this place or not. I was still not very sure of my parent's intention but later I thought that maybe because I am the apple of their eyes they to some extent wanted me to stay here. But they never expressed that to me explicitly, thinking that it may become an obstacle in my way of preparations to go to England. Meanwhile a group of my friends who already went to Newcastle started telling me to go there soon. I was in a complete dilemmatic situation. When I was almost at the verge of leaving for Newcastle there came an unexpected turn in my mind.

I myself also don't know when I fell in love with the place. There are multiple factors behind that; the list is pretty long. Firstly the college campus is extremely beautiful and spacious with extended green lawns and meadows. And the best part of our English department is our professors. All of them are super –friendly to us. Our department is known as the 'coolest department.' The most important thing is that they never made us consider English as a subject rather they compelled us to think English as the mirror reflecting the stories of our life and society in the truest form .And thus I got engrossed within their lectures and thus I started seeing English in a different way. While Asijit sir's modernism teaching led us to question our existence and existence of God's presence, Anisha maam's teaching of a great epic like 'Iliad' conquered me completely. And Literature can be so captivating sometimes, that I decided to stay here and continue my studies in this college only. And within a very short time I realized one thing that I didn't make a mistake. I decided to postpone my venture to Newcastle and informed the university authorities to cancel my accommodation booking and my CAS number also. It was indeed a tough decision for I extremely love England and there we have a group also where I informed my decision that I have planned not to go to England leaving Heritage.

It was my dream from my childhood to have a playground in my school. But places like Lake Gardens or Southern Avenue are one of the busiest and highly congested places in Kolkata. So my school buildings were always sandwiched within the concrete jungles of the city. That dream came true in my college ,our college is surrounded with many playgrounds and lawns where we spent some of the best of my moments with my friends. I'm an extremely sports loving person and often I used to play badminton with my friends in those fields during free periods. Our classroom was at the top floor .Through the windows , I could see the green playground of Heritage school where little kids used to play. There were big trees beside our classrooms, and sometimes during sudden gusts of winds the boughs of the trees almost came near our hands. Nature was at her fullest in the campus. Literature when gets mingled with nature, it truly creates a different aura.

One day I remember probably in the month of October, soon after our college reopened after Durga Puja holidays suddenly the clouds started gathering and ultimately bursted out into heavy showers. That rainfall was due to the retreating monsoon which in Bengali we call 'Ashiner jhor'.I along with my friends were sitting in the cafeteria at that time when the rain came. It was around 2pm.Now, from this cafeteria is adjacently located right besides our college building. But we have to walk two steps to enter into the college.We had a class from 2pm that day. But we weren't in a mood of doing the class that time. Watching the rainfall through the fronds of the lemon green palm leaves, and drops of rain which trickled down the leaves of the palm trees gave me an immense pleasure to my eyes. Rains are not just showers from Heaven but rain can also be wondrous, rains can also be awe-inspiring and such feelings I experienced in my nerves while I watched the rain with my dearest friends Oishee,Salwa and Sneha.There came a smell of 'gorom cha'(tea) to my nose when one of our canteen staffs added roasted tea leaves within the boiling water which stimulated all my senses and I savored the smell of soil mixed with rain.

All these simple casual things, like experiencing an Autumn's afternoon showers or that tree whose boughs provided us an extra breath of freshness by nodding its head sometimes during warm days, would'nt have got a significance in my mind,if covid wouldn't have arrived and separated us from our college.

The pain of separation from such a lovely spot is just unbearable. Those moments ,those familiar smells ,those regular lectures which took us to a different world all proved their own importance when covid took over the control from our hands. It has turned all the familiar into unfamiliar and I then started understanding that what I had got was a bliss which I miss at every moment today.

# MEMORIES OF WOME'S DAY CELEBRATION

The women's day celebration is indeed one of the best memories of my very short period of offline college days. Just two days before, the women's day, Anisha ma'am came to the morning class and she said, "Our College is going to celebrate women's day this year .So I will urge everyone to take part in the event." All of us remained silent. Every time ,we are almost requested by our professors to keep silence but when we are asked to do something productive we becomes silent. Not because, we weren't willing to participate but because we start thinking exactly what to do .She realized our mental state. Anisha ma'am started picking up some of our names. Now before I will say why she picked me up for reciting a poem in that event because just on the previous day we had a poetry reading session in one of our classes conducted by Rituparna ma'am. I recited a Bengali poem by Rabindranath Tagore. So I received a handsome amount of applause and appreciation. So hearing that ,she liked it and asked me to recite a poem. Not just me but many of my classmates were asked to recite poems related to women's empowerment while a few others went for dancing and singing .And the next two days it was a crazy preparations. While on one hand ,we had the preparations for our various presentations ,on the other hand there got engaged a group of students to decorate the walls of the hall with paintings ,colored ribbons and balloons. For the two days of preparations we weren't in a mood of studying because of the excitement. For celebrations were associated with the funs and a little bit of freedom from the hard and fast routine of classes. We were often sneaking off into the hall on the excuse of decorating or preparing it for the program. Our professors knew well our real motives behind the apparent motives of room decoration, but they never scolded us. Our college is almost like a semi-school. Everyone is so vigilant and caring to us that, there was almost no way to miss classes without any proper reason.

And then came the day of our program. It was a Friday. We being the participants arrived a little earlier for rehearsing our performances for the final time. Anisha ma'am being the organizer of the whole program was in a state of extreme business. I saw her almost running through the corridors for once she was getting called by the music group ,the very next moment she was getting called by the dance group. The hall got gradually overflowed with huge noises and bustles as people started coming in. There was a small adjacent room beside the hall from where striking sounds from the guitar strings were coming, as the music group was arranging everything before beginning with their performances. I and one of my classmates had a duet performance of recitation of two separate poems knitted in one thread of thought ,that is worshipping the women's power through the incidents of some simple women. At that time also we weren't aware of the fact that it was going to be our last unmasked and unadulterated joy before the pandemic was about to snatch all the happiness and smiles from our hearts and faces and would lead us to an indefinite period of separation. The program reached to its ultimate level of success with Anisha ma'am's fantastic recitation of the poem 'Ami Shei Meye'. Her powerful way of rendition still echoes in my ears and creates a goose-bumps. It was our last offline cultural event that we had in our college.

I was sitting with my best friends some rows behind and we were almost sitting on each other's shoulder as we always used to do while sitting in the class.The greater amusement happened after the program came to an end .We had an endless photo session in various areas of the college by keeping our professors at the middle and we giving poses surrounding them.In these house arrested days when I retrospect that day those unmasked laughters ,those crazy photosessions almost cuddling each other,I terribly wish if we could have stopped the time there . This pandemic has just not taught us social distancing from people but a distanced way of living away from our favorite places and just live on memories. It was indeed one of the best days in my short offline college life. Through such an occasion the teacher-student became more intimate.But the most important thing that I learned from there was that all women's empowerment should take place not for the equality of women to men but for the equity of women to man.I learned that men shouldn't be considered as the frame of reference for judging women's development.Rather the college program made me learn that men and women must be kept in one standard . 'Each for equity not equality.'

# FINDING THE BEST FRIENDS

"Love is flower like, Friendship is like a sheltering tree."- Coleridge. How much true this statement is I realized that during these hard times. Heritage has gifted me with such an excellent group of friends without whom I am pretty sure, I wouldn't have been able to survive this terribly lonesome days. The pandemic has taught us once again the worth of friendships by separating us for an unlimited time. But our friendship developed in a much permutation-combination way. Some came, some went, some retained, some left and thus, it created a new set of friendship that is 'college friendship'. On the first day of our college, I went a little earlier and was standing on the backward side of our reception hall, from where the school ground can be seen. It is almost like a small balcony and I was watching the children of the Heritage school were playing among them while a enjoying a soothing breeze that was blowing. A few moments later a tall and stout statured girl came and stood beside me. Suddenly my eyes turned at her .She were so tall that I almost gazed at her for a few moments and then she started the conversation first. "Do you know where is our first year class going to take place?" I asked her, "I too am in first year, so neither I know the routine nor I know the classroom."And after a few seconds, I asked her, "From where you have purchased this shade of eyeliner?"As I am a great lover of eyeliners that's my favorite makeup product by the way, so the bluish shade eyeliner that she applied on her eyes on that day, caught my attention. She replied me, "It's Lakme absolute shade eyeliner."And thus with all these chitchats, she became my best friend named Oishee.And from that silly eyeliner discussion our friendship rolled and rolled and reached at a great height.One incident that I think one of the best, the most adventurous and at last one of the funniest incidents of us together was entering into college in time by galloping a long wire fence. Here I need to mention one thing as our college is having an enormous campus, almost every day it seemed to us that why the college didn't have an arrangement of a small auto or a bus to pick us from the main gate of the college and drop us in front of the college, so that it could save time and also we didn't have to walk such a long path, when we had a haste to attend a class. So most of us acquired a short-cut route to enter the college. There was a narrow space beside the school playground which would lead us to the college in a bit lesser time. But as the ground fell within the school campus, just to keep it separate from the college campus there was a long wire fence, surrounding the ground. The fence had two gates also which most of the times remained opened. But unfortunately, that day both the gates were locked. It was a Monday, and the first class was from 9. 30AM .I usually was never late to the college except some very few cases. It was in of those very few days ,when unfortunately I was late. As I was entering into the main gate of the college ,I met with Oishee and another of my classmates. The three of us were almost running for it was 9.25 A.M by our watch. We walked hastily through the narrow pavement of that ground and as we reached in front of the fence gate ,we were almost shocked. To our utter surprise ,we saw that the fence gate was locked. A large lock was hanging at the latch of the both the gates. We looked at our watch ,it was then 9.27 A.M.There was not a single security guards to whom we could ask to come and open the lock .We starred at each other for a while. The third friend who was there with us told us , "I am returning back the same route and will enter from the front of the college."Now returning back would have taken at least 10 minutes more time to enter into the class. Oishee asked me , "What should we do right now?",I thought for a while and told her , "Let us gallop this wire fence somehow." With widened eyes and open mouth ,she asked me , "What! How you will climb the fence and gallop it ?' I also felt a bit nervous for it was a quite a long fence almost 10-12 feet tall. But I am always a bit adventure loving fellow. I said her, "Oishee let me climb the fence and go to the other side ,then you'll come. She told me, "Are you sure ?Whether you'll be again to it?"But I was determined to experience the crazy adventure of crossing the long fence. It was indeed a hard task for me because I am not a very tall person .But still taking up the challenge I first took off my shoes and started slowly climbing up the wire fence. Holding and balancing my body against the wire I slowly climbed up and reached the top of the fence. She was still afraid for the wire was almost shaking slightly with my weight. Then gathering a little more courage ,I again climbed down on the other side of the fence and ultimately when I found the ground nearer to my foot I jumped down and finally landed on the other side in front of our college safely. Then I said to Oishee , "Now it's your turn."Both of us laughed at each other from the opposite sides and the watch struck at 9.30 A.M.I told her, "Hurry up nothing will happen ,its almost time."She one by one threw mine and her bags ,then the pairs of shoes and started gradually climbing up the wire. It was a bit easier for her to climb up the fence for she is quite taller then me. She also followed the same way ,but when she was half the way ,I started palpitating. For the wire fence was not a very durable and hard one. The full wire fence was rapidly shaking and I became a bit nervous .But anyway ,suppressing all the nervousness and palpitations inside ,I started telling her, "Carefully climb down ,don't hurry." Ultimately she also could land on the other side of the fence in front of our college. Both of us sighed a deep sigh of relief. It was really a great adventure and one of the most memorable way of beginning a day in the college. We then wearing our shoes and taking the bags on our shoulder ,we hurried for the class. Now certainly we can't have such adventurous and funny experiences but I still laugh at my loudest sitting alone in my room thinking of my crazy plans and adventures and she was always a partner and a supporter of all my craziness.

Another best incident of us that I keep remembering every time ,when I am sitting idle in my room alone thinking of reading some new books was getting the National Library membership card. It was a Sunday morning. It was around first week of March 2020 and it was a lazy weekend morning. Being a literature student ,I sometimes feel like reading some old classics which are out of our syllabus. And I asked my dad of making a library card so that I can read any types of books whatever I want to read out f my syllabus. Suddenly I asked him, "Should I make a National Library's membership card? It will be helpful isn't it ? Ma was sitting beside me, she said , "Yes it will be great if you can have a National Library's membership card .You'll have a great time to read sitting there." I immediately picked up my phone and called Oishee and told my whole plan and said, "Okay fine I am also coming." She without even thinking for a second time ,immediately accepted the proposal. For her it was more of accompanying me than making a membership card. But the National Library membership card was literally a disaster. On Sunday afternoon we went there and from my house it takes almost two or two and half hours to reach National Library. I was a little late in arriving there. She arrived a bit earlier. That day, we mostly roamed around the whole area of National Library as the place is absolutely rich with a verdant freshness for its enormous greenish fields. There we sat beneath a huge banyan tree which has reached at its ripe old age. The old building standing at the centre of the whole area with it massive old white pillars as the symbol bearing the British Heritage of architecture. Both of us entered into the main building of National Library. It has been turned into a beautiful museum and the first thing we saw entering there was a statue of the great Prince Dwarakanath Tagore. As we entered into the museum we felt amused to see the wonderful paintings and some of the exotic specimens of books and a lot more things. I told her, " Just imagine we were not even aware of the fact that there is such a beautiful museum within National Library ." It was quite a warm afternoon. For the maintenance of the vintage building of the pre Independent period the National Library's books and reading rooms have been shifted to another building opposite to the main building ,it is called

'Bhasha Bhawan.' We went there and told the receptionist the purpose of our coming. We were asked to sit and wait there inside. We were having our college Id card with us fortunately and was given a registration form which needed to be filled and signed by our principal sir. We were super-excited to go inside the library hall but usually they don't allow anybody without the library card to go inside. But somehow they could able to believe us by seeing our faces apparently ,for at time ,people's faces didn't remain covered with the mask of fear that we were innocent fellows just excited to see the book collection of the library. We love the pin drop silence atmosphere of the library ,almost we could hear our heart beats. That day went like that. At that also we were absolutely ignorant of the upcoming funny disaster that was about to come to us for getting the membership card. We planned to fill the form and get it signed by our principal sir the next day within the college hours. But for some reasons we couldn't meet with principal sir ,for he was busy with a seminar. So we went to find our HOD.But sir didn't come to the college that day for he went to Ahmedabad at that time for some works.Atlast, we went to Anisha ma'am for getting our library forms signed by her, and she readily signed both our forms. That day in the afternoon we went to National Library with the hope of getting done with our membership card which was completely an illusion. We went there and entered into the office to submit the form. The office staff took the forms from our hands and said, "This form is not valid for it doesn't have an office seal." None of us noticed that we need an office seal for its mandatory in that form. Both of us with a sense of disappointment came out from there. I asked Oishee,

"What to do now?" She thought for a while and told me, "There's a Flurrys on the opposite side of the library. Let's go there and have something." How happy and carefree were those days when we didn't fear to enter into any enclosed shops, or our hands didn't have any smells of sanitizers! So we went there and were initially puzzled what to have for all those confectionaries were so delicious that we almost wanted to eat all of them.Atlast she told me, "Let's have a donut."So we ordered for a donut and she took a glass of cold coffee which we shared together. And those days are now to us the happiest memories of sharing the best times together. And ending with the last sip of the coffee we for that day went back to home with a hope and determination of getting the membership card the next day. The next day, we went to our principal sir and got the stamp from him and again ventured to National Library .By the time we reached there, it was their lunch break. So the office staff went to have his lunch. We were told to wait. After waiting for 45 minutes I got restless. I told her, "I am feeling bored sitting here in the reception idle like this." So she took me out to the green lawns and both of us laid there on the soft green grasses. We could see rays of sun was peeping through the leaves of the tree under which we laid together. We were crazy clicking some pictures together to get rid of the boredom. Now today ,when we are completely locked up in houses I look at those pictures and feel that those moments which we once called boring timeless hours have gifted us with the best memories when we had stayed and passed hours after hours together ,laid anywhere ,sat everywhere without the fear of constantly spraying sanitizer for there wasn't any covid to haunt us constantly. Those futile moments ,those crazy unnecessary photo sessions those walking and roaming together all proved their own significance and importance to us by putting us into this challenging situation. After almost one hour we again went but that staff still was not there at his desk. So again we went out and I being a huge lover of gardens and flowering plants ,started seeing those countless number of flower tubs bearing petunia ,marigold ,poppy ,some other beautiful flowers whose names are not known to me.The atmosphere is an ideal spot for studying. There didn't reach any bustles and commotions of city life, no traffic horns but silence is the only ornament of that place. We listened to the birds' song and almost went into a state of drowsiness for it was a warm day but the cool shadowy bower of the enormous trees gave us a soothing effect. After half an hour, we went inside and finally found that office staff and we submitted our forms to him. He told us to come a few days later to get our membership card. A few days later in the afternoon from the college we went there. Now, our bus dropped us at a wrong place and we started walking from there to reach National Library. We got confused for in Belvedere Road ,the alleys look so identical with bougainvillea trees almost at every turn that getting confused we walked the same path twice for it was like a loop. I at one point stopped and told her, "I think that we have lost our way and have been walking the same alley twice." She was also confused ,for both of us were absolutely novice about the place and there we couldn't find a road map also. Actually it was the mistake made by the Google map. It was showing the direction for car and there are certain roads which are one way. So it showed us to walk twice the same path and to reach that place. We were badly sweating for it was almost the middle of March and in Kolkata from February end only ,the sun starts shinning at its maximum acridity so to make all our dresses get drenched with perspiration. But in spite of feeling extremely fatigued while the sun was almost sucking the last bit of remaining water from within us, we still enjoyed that walking. We laughed at each other for our foolishness ,but none of us expressed the slightest of our disgust to one another, for we were happy to spend the pure joy of walking miles after miles together. While walking past the Greek Consulate house ,I saw a pink bougainvillea almost overshadowing half of the alley .The pink flowers had almost has spread a pink carpet on the road. The vicinity was like a pacific thoroughfare and I picked up a bougainvillea flower and continued our walking. Finally after walking for almost forty-five minutes we could find the main road. From there we fortunately got an auto which saved from our never-ending walk of that day. Soon we entered and that much awaited moment came when he gave the membership card to us. Both of us, for the first time got the chance to see and feel the essence so many books by touching them. Especially from the very old books ,I could get that typical vintage smells and the brownish pages which filled my mind with ecstacy.We savored the maximum pleasure of the library talked about various types of books,we kept on calling each other every now and then telling, "Look at this book ,that one is amazing isn't it?" That day we continued doing this till 4.30 pm when we planned of returning home for we were felt tired and National Library is quite a long distance from both of our houses.

And that was the end of book reading and going to

National Library for it was just the next week when the pandemic outbreak took place and the government declared to shut down all the educational institutions along with gave the order to keep all the libraries, shopping malls and restaurants closed.We never knew that those long walks ,those paths which we traversed together would become our best memories of being together before we got separated away by the rapid spreading o the pandemic.Visiting National Library together for the membership card and then sneaking off into Flurrys a thousand times has become one of the most memorable incident.The pandemic outbreak and our separation and these weird changes that has come in our lives have made this incident to me.Those were the memories of our unmasked smiles ,sanitizers free days.

Now a days when I talk to her, maybe our discussion topics have changed ,the tone of our conversation has got tinged with sadness and a sense of missing those moments and mostly the conversation is how to live on just memories but these incidents of galloping wire fence or National library visit still brings joys to our hearts. Oishee has been my constant company to all my crazy sudden demands of going here and there doing something childish. We often have endless demands on some literature pieces, and our late night conversations starting from nothing to everything, she has always been there, just not in front of me but virtually we still continue to create memories which will be our fuel for combating with despair filled days till we see the new dawn of hope and a disease free world.

The two of our friendship turned into a friend circle when two more came and joined us. And after our friend circle got enlarged by the addition of the two more fellows ,the four of us were always seen together in the college. The four of us became so inseparable that in spite of the sweating badly we used to sit in one bench, almost on each other's shoulder. I don't know whether we'll ever get back this chance of sitting so close to each other. For pandemic at that time there was no fear of disease and we never even imagined of sitting separately. So the two more fellows were Salwa and Sneha.Salwa and I were from the same school but we never talked in the school for she was in Humanities and I was in Science stream. One night at around 10pm I got a whatsapp message from Salwa. It was written, "I this is Salwa, and I want to get some guidance from you regarding the admission procedure of your college for I am also interested to take admission at The Heritage College." Initially I took a few minutes to remember who was this for I had seen her in my English tuition but just by her face not by her name. But seeing the whatsapp profile picture I could able to recognize her. I replied her back with the maximum amount of informations and guidance which I knew about.A few days later, I again got a message from her, she wrote, "I have finally got the admission at your college.Will meet you tomorrow in the class." I was happy to hear this, I just texted her back writing "Congratulation." And the next day when she and I met each other in the class, I called her to the bench where Oishee and I were sitting. And that's when, from our friendship from two became three.

After a few weeks later, a cute fair girl with a bit of Nepalese face cutting .She was sitting quietly at a corner of a bench. We were not very sure in which language we should speak to her. So for a few days we just saw her in the class very calm in nature, but we didn't talk to her. One morning, I was arrived a little bit early to the class and was sitting alone. It was raining outside. I after sitting quietly for some seconds went beside the window to watch the rain. I stretched out my hands outside to touch and feel the beautiful rain drops. Once a big drop of rain fell on my hand and at that moment I had to turn around for I could hear a footstep inside the classroom. That girl came and she herself started the conversion, "This rain has made all the roads muddy, it's so annoying." She also added, "Kolkata is a very congested city, in the place from where I am coming, it's much cleaner." I asked her, "From where are you coming?" She replied, "I'm from Coochbehar." And then our gossip continued till the point our professor entered into the class and we had to stop our gossip for the time being .And from her conversation I could realize one thing that she is a pure Bengali and she was badly missing her home town. Soon Salwa and Oishee came into the class I introduced her to them telling, "See this is Sneha the newest addition to our friend circle." And from there we became a group of four. From then till the day our college went for a shut down we had always remained together during the college hours. Starting from our canteen gossips to the four of us watching the rains together, our friendship escalated in a pretty fast way.

One thing that I must mention here is the biggest key of having a stability in friendship id that the mutual believe on each other and to retain purity of the friendship. During these days, when pandemic has distanced us physically but still it has failed to distance us mentally. This pandemic has taught us how much it is essential to have a good friend circle to whom you can share all your emotions no matter how much grave or silly they are.

# MEMORIES WITH PROFESSORS

Our college life literally seems to me like a history to me now days and those beautiful moments of our college classes seem like the best memories which I will bear in my heart as the snippets of those happy unmasked college days. But within that small period of barely eight months, I have found and got a lot more than what I never even dreamed of getting.

There exist some people in this universe who do have the talent of getting admixed with you in such a way, surpassing all the formal boundaries that you'll feel compelled to add that person into the list of your favorite persons .Regardless any age or educational qualifications ,these types of people come suddenly to our lives just to break all the old wrong notions of our mind and instead making us learn that 'True education never gives birth to a ruling attitude inside your mind rather it gives birth to a sheltering tree like person under whose shade the world will seek shelter."And Heritage has truly gifted me with such a professor like this.

"Professors can hardly be good, professors can hardly be caring." During the end of our school life we used to hear such words from our teachers. I will not go for a critical analysis of this statement because to me this statement proved itself to be completely wrong. Not just the friendship which has got more intensified when the pandemic came and distanced us but also it has intensified the teacher-student relationship. Pandemic has taught us the mutual necessity and bonding of between teachers and students.

Re-writing the old definitions are tough but if you have the power in your heart and believe in your work, you can bring the change. Just like creating a new record by breaking the old records are hard, likewise re-defining something by breaking the age old definition is also extremely tough. But those who can create a definition are indeed great in a way. And that's what Professor Anisha Sen did. She redefined the whole definition of a professor to us. This long separation from the college has given me the chance to know her in a much deeper way, not just a professor, but as a friend, philosopher and guide.

On the second day of our college Anisha ma'am came into the class. The first thing that caught my eyes was her habitual simplicity. There was not the slightest of any classy attitudes that was there within her appearance rather she was a very cheerful, friendly young personality. She started the class by addressing us not as 'Students' but by the term 'My kids. 'And in the next one hour also she never uttered the words students to address her. This natural way of giving us a quick cozy effect was something that I liked the most. But the most interesting thing that attracted all of our attention was that when she told that, "You'll feel very amused to know that I am doing my research on a topic which is our entire favorite." She stopped for a few seconds to see the spark of curiosity within our eyes and then she again started, "My PhD topic is fairy tales." Hearing this I felt extremely delighted and surprised. From that day onwards I started calling her my fairytale professor. That day it went just as an introductory class and she didn't start teaching us on that day.

The next day when it was our turn to introduce ourselves to her, I could slightly get the tinge of her sense of humor from her conversations with us. There a boy in our class who said that he tried to get into medical but he failed and then took up English honors as his subject. Anisha ma'am smiled at him and said, "Okay so we do have a doctor among us and incase of any medical emergencies he will be there for rescuing us." And the boy along with the whole class laughed at this joke. It's a bit hard to get hold of her sense of humor because it's a so sharp but subtle that often people will fail to get hold of it.

Anisha ma'am started her lecture on the third day but in a different way. I still remember the special way with which she started her class. She instead of going into the syllabus directly, she started her teaching with figures of speech .Now it somehow invoked a question within our minds behind her reason of teaching figures of speech. But I very quickly could realize one thing that ,we came from school with a wrong notion that we have a huge knowledge in figures of speech for we have read the very famous book named 'Wren and Martin' for English grammar and we solved all the back questions of it and we know them well. As Anisha ma'am gradually started explaining the innumerable figures of speeches apart from just similes, metaphors and ironies, I slowly got engrossed within her lecture. No sooner did she proceed with her lessons than my misconception of knowing all the figures of speech got broken. But the thing which I realized after she ended the class was that I couldn't even understand from where and how one hour passed away. And today at this situation I terribly want to get back to that class which never even let me realize that from where and how an hour had passed. In these house arrested days those classes are some of the sweetest memories which I cherish and can find pleasures. It was in that class where Anisha ma'am taught oxymoron. And she asked examples from us on this oxymoron. I in a little chuckle some manner told her, "Ma'am I do have a good example, that is regularly irregular students. That word regularly irregular is also an oxymoron."She could realize that it was intended for fun. She laughed hearing this and told me "This example is too good to be written on the board." She stopped for a second and said, "Keep this example just within us." And both of us laughed once again. And this I remember as one of the best and funniest moments of my college days and also Anisha ma'am's class.

There were more such funny and mischievous incidents which bring a breath of freshness to my mind when I recall them. Another such incident was that when I bunked Anisha ma'am's class one day. It was a Tuesday. I did not go anywhere missing her class simply I returned home back a little earlier for the sake of getting a bit more time for self-studying for it was just a week left before our first semester exam began. On Tuesday we had Anisha ma'am's class after the lunch break. And suddenly what happened in my mind I don't know what I never did I did that day. I missed that class. The actual story happened the next day. Anisha ma'am came into the class opened the register book and started calling our names. To my utter surprise she stopped a second before calling my name and then asked, "Where were you yesterday dear?" I with a baffling eyes thinking about one thing that how much observant she was on us that she out of so many students observed me for missing a class for a single day. But the most salient thing which I compelled me to say the truth was her attitude. Her way of questioning me was so gentle and it was never intended for scolding me. I developed such a believe on her that I immediately told her my cause of going home back earlier without fabricating any false stories of illness or fever. And when I remember this incident later it just invoked one thought in my mind that creating a space of assurance and comfort in student's mind is not an easy task. But Anisha ma'am gave us such a place that we never even think of acquiring any shield of making up stories for giving justifications to our larks in front of her. Later when I think of all those larks that we did during our college hours I laugh at my loudest. And also feel thankful to Anisha ma'am for being a little lenient with us in these matters. I could realize one thing later that on the first day of our orientation program it was said to all of us that Heritage takes care of each and every student and keeps a keen observation on them, like it happens in our homes. And she really justified that line. It was not just Anisha ma'am but with our other professors also the thing remains the same.

I remember another funny incident like this. People are usually reluctant with the general subject classes. So that day, some of us went to our cafeteria to have cold coffee. And cold coffee to us was an addiction especially during times when we did not feel like doing a class but we were afraid of getting scolded if we miss it. It was our sociology class. So before entering into the class, a group of our friends planned of having cold coffee for it was a hectic day with three back to back English honors classes. And we did so. And while we came near the elevator, two of my friends suddenly told each other, "Hey I am not in a mood of doing this sociology class today."The other friend replied, "Who loves to do sociology classes?" And the next moment we all turned our heads to enter into the elevator, we say sociology ma'am.All of us got such a mixed feeling that we all burst out into laughter including our sociology ma'am.She also laughed at us saying, "Hmm who loves to do sociology classes?" And we all laughed out once again and entered into our lift. The two of them ran away in fear of getting scolded from behind. But ma'am didn't scold them later also when they came back. That was one of the most hilarious moments which I remember from my offline college days.

But from all these months I could have enjoy my classes offline, I learned innumerable things which have helped me a lot during these hard times. Firstly the good memories of the classes and the classroom which not only just taught us those mere poems and stories but she actually taught us to see literature and relate it to our lives. Literature is the mirror of our insight and also of the societal condition during which it was composed.

Another incident that will remain significant to me forever was that I could see the wide spectrum of literature. It was in our second semester we had a paper on Indian English literature. I was never fond of Indian English literature maybe because from my childhood I grew up reading only British literature classics. So I felt a bit unhappy to know that we had to study Indian English literature. One day I went to Anisha ma'am and told her, "I don't at all like Indian English literature, what is that all about?" She asked me, "What's the reason behind your dislike?" I innocently replied to her, "Because I don't find the sweetness and the charm of the green valleys, golden daffodils or nightingale's sweet songs references in Indian English literature." She smiled and said, "Literature is not just the dreamy imaginations of beautiful landscapes, it also deals with the grim realities of life." And I then asked her, "But what is the purpose of reading those poetries which can't invoke a sweet aura within my mind and give freshness to my soul?" And that conversation escalated to a level of literary debate of which one to call better 'Indian English' or 'British English'. And at last Anisha ma'am when saw that I will not agree to her call Indian English as also a good ,she stopped me telling , "Okay wait for some days until I start teaching the poem, and I will also see whether you'll stick to this idea or it gets changed." So the debate ended up almost with a note of that whether she could able to make me love Indian English literature through her teachings or not.

And a few days later I came to a conclusion that there really exist some teachers in this universe, who are such great engineers that they can engineer over the minds of the students and can give birth to a new idea in their minds. And this what Anisha ma'am did .I started gradually believing that she has a capacity of making those literary pieces my favorite which I were once in the list of dislikes. But apart from just making them favorite, her teachings made me realize that how literature can be linked with our lives.

My Indian English literature reading started off with a poem called 'Our Casuarina Tree' by Toru Dutt.After giving the brief details of Toru Dutt's life, Anisha ma'am began the poem. The more she proceeded with her teachings, the more I started linking with my life. She once told in the class, 'That every little objects in our lives can be symbolic and significant.' Like this Casuarina tree which was not just a tree but was actually the symbol of holding all the memories. And then I started linking it with my life and I said to myself, 'Yes it is true indeed. 'As to me also, there was such a mango tree under which I used to play with my friends during childhood .In the summer, we used to throw small stones to the mangoes which used to hung high above the boughs. In most of the summer evenings, it was our game to pick mangoes from that tree and often we got scolded by the security guards of our complex for trying to climb high above the mango trees without even knowing how to climb. I along with some my friends used to hold each other one above another's shoulder and make a long chain to get the mangoes within our reach but every time we failed for we couldn't even reach of the height of the mangoes. And one day I remember a young boy of around 20 came and climbed up the tree and picked some mangoes and smoothly came down the tree. He handed each one of us two three mangoes and we felt extremely happy on that day.

As years passed, all those childish naughtiness, all those desires of doing particularly those things which were forbidden gradually got volatilized. All our friends got scattered here and there and mostly we got engaged deeply with our studies. That mango tree to also bears such sweet memories of our carefree days and our lost and scattered friendships. And after Anisha m'am could make me savor the flavor of the poem I gradually started loving Indian English literature.

I learned from there that the best way of understanding

literature is to link it with our lives and the incidents of our lives. Another poem of Nissim Ezekiel named 'Enterprise' where the poet talked about the hypocrisy of pilgrimage. I instantly remember of a story that I heard of this unsuccessful pilgrimage and the heckles that they faced where God was on one side and the pilgrims were on other side, trying to just survive by escaping from that pilgrimage spot. It was indeed a funny incident and quite relatable to Ezekiel's 'Enterprise'. When I was young I heard of a story about pilgrimage disaster from one of my cousin's grandma. She along with some of her friends once went to 'Ganga sagar mela.' It's a pilgrimage that takes place every year in Ganga sagar island where Hindu pilgrims from various parts of the world and also foreign tourists come to take a holy dip in the River Ganges as they believe that this dip can purify their souls and body.So my grandma and her friends went there in a group. Firstly when they reached their they couldn't see the actual sea of water; instead they saw the sea of people. It almost seemed to them that the world had gathered there. On the day of the occasion, they couldn't find the slightest space in the water to have dip .The water and the whole area soon become so filthy and stink. The group of my grandma and her friends faced so terrific obstacles that they thought of coming home quickly to find God within their souls and home and not to find God by going to pilgrimage. And this was what I could find while reading Ezekiel's 'Enterprise'. The last line of the poem was, 'Home is where we have to gather grace.' That's what happened to them also. It brought me back the memory of the story that I heard from my cousin's grandma for she is no more alive. So the more, I could relate the Indian English literature with myself or the stories I heard, it started coming close to my heart.

But the unfortunate thing was, by the time Anisha ma'am reached half way with teaching Ezekiel the colleges went for a shut down. So we learned half of the poem in the offline classes and half in the online mode. But I started liking Indian English to such an extent that I one day told Anisha ma'am, "Yes you were right that day. Indian English literature can also be fantastic and you almost made it my favorite."The one thing that I understood that literature is not about finding reason behind each and everything but to search for getting the connection with you. In these house arrested days, I learned one thing that not just my friends who have contributed to make the happy and funny memories but our professors also hold an important place in our minds to gift us such amazing memories.

One thing I must say that pandemic has given me the opportunity to see literature in a new light. She has taught us that how academics need to be taught in the most collaborative way. She once told in the class that, "True academics never teaches us discrimination rather it teaches us to become non-judgmental and impartial and collaborative."And I felt it later that, it's only the academics which have kept all these people bound in a same string. I terribly miss those memories of learning, imagining and thinking about the massive power of literature while sitting within the classroom during these bleak days.

# CLASSES TURNED ONLINE

After getting trapped within the world of mobiles and laptops we all created a sentence that is, "The whole life has itself become online." And these online classes gradually become a part of our day to day life. After the pandemic engulfed all our funs, happiness and larks, our only means of getting connected to our classmates and professors together are the online classes. No matter how much hectic or boring the online mode of education is but I think without this slightest connection, we would have forgotten each other in this one and half year of separation and still its continuing.

Initially, when the pandemic started we fell surprised when we first heard of online classes. For none of us ever experienced what is online mode of studying. But a few days later when it really started, I think we honestly get back some purpose of our life, or rather it saved us from suffering into severe existential crisis. It actually brought a routine to our temporal eventless disorganized life. Indeed teaching and learning in online mood is tough but still we have to live in the present.

Coming out from the cacoon of memories, at this present moment for us online classes is the only means of our confluence .It is almost like a distanced happiness. Certainly there is always a gap in the online mode of education but still that's the only bridge between all of us. When these proposals of taking online classes were declared by the government, we weren't very sure of how to learn and follow such lectures and teachings. I remember, both our professors and us were in a state of absolute condition from where and how to begin with the syllabus. Anyway by breaking all our dilemmas when our professors started the online classes, it truly brought some newness within our monotonous days.

Gradually we started getting accustomed with this online teaching mode. I must say that we must be thankful to our laptops and mobiles or tabs for giving us such faithful service and helping us to virtually meet with each other. There happen various funny incidents in online classes. Either someone's audio is getting on while someone is teaching, the next moment someone's video is getting on, but we can't see the face of the person just can see the fan rotating at a full speed on the ceiling. If somebody has a pet in his or her house and the audio has suddenly got on, instead of hearing that person's sound we can hear the pet dogs barking sound. And our professors instead of scolding or expressing the slightest disgust start laughing and enjoying the fact that the pets are also interested in online classes.

It almost seems to us like a home-schooling where the educational institutions are at our homes. Initially when it started I really missed the classroom feelings the noisy classrooms, all of our bustling together till the point our professors walked into the class and shut the door and told the class to become silent. Now in the online classes everything is silent no sounds, no bustling. Here the situation has turned opposite, it's just a deathly silence till our professors enter into the meeting and start the class.

I never expected that online classes can be good. But it happened in the most unexpected way that gradually the online classes become a part a part of our lives and we started liking it gradually. It was in these online classes where my critical way of thinking about a literature enhanced. As we are told to think on some particular poems or stories, we critically analyze and think over the matter and our reply only confirms our presence in the class. And slowly by doing this, I learned how to interpret literature in various ways. That's where the wide expansion of literature lies.

And literature does not have an age limitation. That's what I learned when Anisha m'am did Sukumar Ray's 'Abol Tabol' with us. I felt surprised to know that those poems which we learned in our childhood days as just the poems of rhymes and humor are not just that. It's a subtle mocking to the society and its follies and vices. In these extreme boring days, I got a chance to look back to those books, those poems and stories which I once thought as just bedtime stories or stomach aching laughter poems.

But it was in these online classes where I learned about Shelley. I being an ardent lover of romantic era poems soon found the relevance of the romantic poets thought with the current situation. While reading the poem 'To A Skylark', I too like Shelley wanted to achieve the independence like the skylark which can fly anywhere between heaven and earth. It is exactly this current situation which has taught me to once again return back to nature and to call nature as the supreme power.

In our online classes also sometimes ,we have such

interesting discussions that we usually don't want to end the class. We sometimes want to take a one day break from our at a stretch studying for two or three long weeks. And mostly we make our requests to Anisha ma'am for we never a get a holiday from her. It is almost like a one chance in a million cases where we have a holiday from Anisha ma'am.And that's why if one day we make a request to her for a break she has to keep it. But I will say we almost never heard a no from her .And those days of our breaks becomes the best for we usually have a poetry reading or a story reading sessions where we read some of the stories or poems which are out of the syllabus. It's a better way of getting entertained in these days of perpetual boredom.

It was just before the Durga puja in 2020 that our college arranged an online program of welcoming the Durga puja the biggest festival of the Bengali's.It was a new way of celebrating or welcoming Goddess Durga in an online mode by doing small cultural performances to celebrate the new normal Durga puja.

The online classes are not just the way of keeping a track with our academics but also a point of confluence of course virtually with all our college friends and professors. The funniest part of this online mode of learning was that people are doing online classes from anywhere for the classes are just within their mobiles or tabs. I remember one day, one of friends came to my house with her mother and when I asked her, "How is your online classes going on?" She couldn't stop giggling and told me, "It's going on within the pocket of my jeans."And I too laughed at my loudest thinking that 'College within pocket. 'Another incident I heard that the teacher told someone to switch on the video and as soon as he switched on, everybody could see an extended green valley and blue sky but not the actual person. So the teacher got angry and asked, "Where are you in Mars?" And then he replied he went to hilly area for a small trip and was sitting on the grass while doing the class. There are many such funny incidents that happen in online classes. One thing that became my favorite during Anisha ma'am's online class is Mojo.Its her pet dog that came as a bundle of joy in September last year when it was just a baby of one month .From then, almost every day he comes into the room when ma'am takes our classes and adds a little more joy to our classes everytime.At the initial stage it couldn't climb up at the height of the laptop so just to confirm its presence it barked and that's what we all enjoyed. I have a many of my friends have taken pets during these days for pets almost act like therapeutic doses during the dull days when people are suffering from mental issues. So for us the online classes are never monotonous, there are always something or the other that added some newness to the classes.

But one thing that I always feel that in this online mode of teaching all the teachers and professors are putting a lot of effort in making us understand and know our lessons in the best possible way. Online way of teaching is never an easy job. I am fortunate enough to be at the receiving end that I always have a chance to ask questions to my professors.

One day, when the covid slightly decreased just before the second wave came, I went to the college for some library works. It was for a short time of one month when the colleges and few schools reopened with just the teachers but not the students. Teachers were taking online classes from the college. And that day after my library work was over; I went to attend Anisha ma'am's class. When I sat beside her and saw that how she was taking the class I almost felt confused and surprised to see that how difficult it is to take classes online. After the class ended I asked her, "How you people have been taking the classes for the past one year?" She said, "Now you can understand that how difficult it is." And I said her, "It is so difficult where it almost seems like talking to the wall where you can't even judge that how much we understand for you can't even see us." It's not just for her but it's for the other professors also and for all of them linked with this teaching profession. It has been really a tough time for both the teachers and the students to continue this teaching-learning process through online. But still this online classes are our oxygen. These classes make us feel that what importance academics have in our lives. Real classes are those which will make one to long for it.

# THE KNOWN BECAME THE UNKNOWN

It's not just possible to live on the memories. So I must come to the reality and talk about the current situation, our lives after pandemic. Pandemic has completely changed the way of our lives. My very known city became the very unknown. Not just it affected the students' lives and career but it has negatively impacted all ages and all class of people. During these house arrested days, I often spend my evenings in the roof top of my apartment which is the only place during this pandemic where I can go unmasked and can take a deep breath of fresh air without fear. Every day I climb the ladder and reach at the highest point of the roof just to see that how our busiest city gradually losing its vibrancy becomes almost silent. It almost seems to me that the city has undergone into hibernation and we are all waiting to see our city at the fullest charm and energy just it was before. The traffics decreased abnormally. I tried to look till the farthest point possible to see the or rather to find my old Kolkata, where everything is running, the bus ,the car ,the metro, the auto along with the people. Mostly in these solitary evenings I don't like to see such a motionless Kolkata. Sometimes Instead of calling it pandemic I started calling it a virus-war while looking over the surroundings and atmosphere. It seems to me like a curfew ,that is declared during the wars, when everything is silent, still and motionless. I alone walk on the rooftop throughout the evening while looking at the sunsets. I soon become a sunset maniac. I feel that the sun is my only companion during these solitary evenings. Everyday clicking the dynamic sunset beauty. Every time I look into the round reddish orange ball of the sky, I see its color changes. And I try to capture all the shades of the evening sky's beauty. For I sometimes ask the evening that if it can paint such a huge canvas of the sky so colorfully so why can't it paint the canvas of our hearts and minds which have lost all its colors just because of this virus. Sometimes I think that everything is going on in the right way as before, just our lives have changed in the most unexpected way. And after clicking sunset pictures, I post them in my whatsapp status or in facebook and within a very short time; I could see many people in my known circle started becoming a lover of sunset pictures.

To me the one hour of my evening walk looking at the infinite sky was actually the hour of freedom. It's not just the freedom from the four walls of my flat but the freedom of mind. The thing that I learned from this that solitude creates a new form of companionship. The silence and tranquility of the lavender hued evening, the sights of the birds flying to their nest with the large halo of the sun behind them invokes in my mind a high imagination of the untouchable beauty and freedom. It is almost my return to nature. I don't even remember when I last saw sunset with so much patience for such a long time. This pandemic has made me see those wonders of nature which goes unnoticed to our eyes for we used to be always in a running state before the pandemic came.

The place where I stay is a bit outskirts of the main city so it is comparatively a bit more peaceful area than the hustles of the main city life. So I can clearly hear the voice of the birds in a more intense way than I heard before. It is almost like looking into the familiar things in an unfamiliar way. The change of my evening routine came during the winter months when there was a temporal decrease of the covid cases before the second wave of the pandemic came. I spend the winter evenings by playing badminton with some of the friends of my housing complex. It kind of brought a change to my solitary way of spending evenings and was the point of confluence of so many people together once again after for the first time after pandemic. We arranged for tournaments on some special days and this whole thing brought immense pleasure to us in the midst of the darkness.

# NATURE'S FURY

It was in the month of May in 2020 which taught me that Nature is not just the moisture laden grasses and humming of bees, the preserving nature can also turn into a destroyer at times. It was the cyclone that took place last year in West Bengal and Orissa and parts of South India. The cyclone was named as Amphan by Thailand.It was on 21st May that Amphan hit West Bengal and the other adjoining regions. But it started giving spoilers two three days prior to its arrival. Now in this world of internets and Medias nothing remains unknown to us. Also we must be thankful to the Meteorological department for spreading the awareness and caution before the storm gave us the final bash. I remember, the weather condition started getting deteriorated two days before the actual day. But that time also, we couldn't exactly sense the amount of ferocity with which the storm would come. On the very day of the storm, I remember all our online classes on that day got cancelled for there were severe network issues in various regions. The sky was overcastted and it was raining from the morning. Constantly I could hear the news updates of the storm that was about to hit Kolkata and the coastal areas in the afternoon. In the coastal areas like Digha,Bakkhali,Sunderbans and also in Odisha the media showed live updates of the surging waves of water which were the precursors of the fury of the approaching storm.

Just when the clock struck at 3 o clock, the super cyclone approached in West Bengal.I through my windows saw that how the clouds from the horizon gathered together at the centre of the sky and when the massive gusts of winds started blowing the clouds started twirling at the centre of the sky. The whole area soon got so covered with darkness that it was hard to figure whether it was day or night. Slowly the ferocity of the storm increased and doors started banging and window panes started shaking violently. At one point the door of my room banged so loudly that I feeling extremely afraid closed the door and went to my parent's room. The three of us locked ourselves up into one room and started talking about various things. The internet connections were already lost. The storm's motion and intensity accelerated. At around 5 or 5.30 it reached at the highest extent. All the glass panes of our flat were shaking so violently ,it almost seemed to us that they would all break down into pieces due to this dangerous blow of the wind. The tree tops lashed backward and forward. I sometimes was slightly moving the shutter of the window to see that whether the trees were okay or not. The jamrul tree which is just beside my room was at one moment getting bended and its boughs were almost getting into my window ,but the next moment getting dragged by the force of the Amphan it got bent to the other side and went farthest away from free. The neem tree in front of my balcony was trying its best to keep it held to the ground strongly through its roots. I felt extremely sad and helpless for I couldn't do anything for the birds which couldn't even understand where to take shelter in the tree or inside our houses. The nests were getting broken and the birds became frightened and puzzled started calling at their loudest when the wind was continuing its torture over the trees and the birds. The three of us stood together and I started praying to God for saving the trees from falling down and the birds from losing their lives and nests. The storm was indeed so furious that maybe I will never find the proper adjective to describe the furious and violent nature of the storm. My parents also for the first time in their lives heard the hissing and whistling mixed sound of the storm. Like a kite which floats in the sky I suddenly saw, an aluminum asbestos twirling high above in the air almost like a kite and it was dangerous. I came close to my mother and said her, "Ma I am very afraid by seeing this devilish storm ,and mostly I am worried with the trees and these birds." Ma was also afraid but she told me, "This storm will not be able to do any harm to your beloved trees and birds." The intensity of the rain rose and water started coming into my room through the little gap under the window shutter.Gradually the floor of my room got covered with water,for we couldn't stop the raindrops to come inside the room.When the cyclone at its full rage was at the mood of almost crushing down the whole world,the glass pane of our washroom got cracked with a great cracking sound and it added to our fear.Ma became so frightened that she started muttering the names of all the Gods and Goddesses to save us from this super cyclone.

And finally after few hours when the cyclone lost half of it's rage ,it gradually started leaving us ,but the rain accompanied with thunder and lightning retained.Very slowly ,the atmosphere started getting cooled down.And me ,baba and ma all three of us looked at each other and said with a sigh of deep relief, "We have finally survived ."Soon after the storm ,I tried to connect with all my friends and acquaintances to know that whether everyone is safe or not. I send whatsapp messages to them.Oishee and I could fially connect over call and she said that the window pane of her kitchen got cracked after banging for thousand times and her kitchen also got flooded with water.

Baba and I started cleaning the water while the electricity connection got lost. The actual suffering started from the next day. There was no electricity connection and our water filter stopped working. We couldn't charge our mobiles and laptops. Just the generator of our complex was working. So we took all our mobiles to the ground floor where there was a plug point which was connected to the generator. All the residents of our blocks started using the multi plugs to charge their mobiles or tabs. This condition continued for three four days. The internet service gradually got restored but in our area as the electricity pole got broken into two halves ,the electricity office couldn't give the electric supply to our area for three four days. For it took time for them to mend the electricity pole and restore the connection. Our neighbours helped us a lot by providing daily the drinking water and also a few times we boiled the tap water cooled it and drank it.
I felt the most anxious for those people who have lost their shelter or those who had their homes near the sea. For after all these problems of water and electricity we at least had the shelter over our heads which many people lost. After a couple days, when we received the newspaper, I felt extremely sad to see the devastating effect of the

super-cyclone. More than the meteorological department's information, it was from the real life experiences of the poor farmers, fishermen who told about have lost their huge loses of home, family members and the saved money. In various parts of the affected areas trees got eradicated, the surging waves of the sea flooded the coastal areas and marooned innumerable people to inaccessible palces.The rescue operators worked at a full swing. The worst thing happened in the College Street area of Kolkata. It is the largest book market in India and is commonly called as 'Boi Para' or the book mart. There the book sellers suffered a loss of lakhs of rupees for uncountable number of books got washed away in this storm. I felt shattered and despaired to think about the huge loss of all these humble class of people. Later I heard from an old lady of our complex that she also had never witnessed such massive and devastating storm ever in her long eighty years of life.

The worst part of the whole incident was that one hand people had already suffered loss of lives and money due to the covid .This super cyclone sprinkle salt on the cut. People were at a loss of what to do, though the government declared ex-gratia to compensate the loses of these poor people.

This was one of the incidents when nature showed its violent form to us but fortunately all the trees in front of my house remained unaffected. I thanked God for listening to my prayers and for saving the trees which are the only shelters of the innocent creatures who live in the trees.

Before the people could recover completely from the damage of Amphan in the same month this year another super-cyclone named 'Yash' struck the areas the same areas and parts of the Digha ,Sunderbans,Sagar island got flooded and houses got swept away. But this time the intensity was slightly less than Amphan but still it caused huge damages in various areas. But this time the Government took more protective measures by taking experiences from Amphan and this time the death cases are almost negligible. In Kolkata there was just rainfall and strong gusts of wind but not that furious that happened during Amphan.

These two furies of nature made us realize that however big and supreme the human beings think of us, Nature is ultimately the supreme power. We do everything to destroy the nature by cutting down the trees and turning every little green spaces into concrete jungles but if Mother Nature becomes furious we will become grains of dust in front of her invincible power. The forces of Nature can be destroyer at times when they try to teach us that Nature is the supreme not we. That's why Wordsworth said, that Nature must be worshipped for she is actual a divine Spirit and also our biggest teacher.

To my survival through these hard times, literature has immense contribution. I now think that, literature works the best when you're sitting alone in your room looking at the outside world but actually looking into your inside. It is during this time when I knew that literature can be our companion not just during the best times of our lives but also during the darkest times of our lives. Literature can give us such an embalming effect that we almost forget the reality within which we're living.

I'm in general a very sensitive child. So I usually read those literature pieces which are thought-provoking in nature. During these days, when I sit alone in my room beside the window, while enjoying the fresh breeze of the jamrul tree beside my window I mostly read stories and poems of nature.

# NATURE,LITERATURE AND PANDEMIC

To my survival through these hard times, literature has immense contribution. I now think that, literature works the best when you're sitting alone in your room looking at the outside world but actually looking into your inside. It is during this time when I knew that literature can be our companion not just during the best times of our lives but also during the darkest times of our lives. Literature can give us such an embalming effect that we almost forget the reality within which we're living.
I'm in general a very sensitive child. So I usually read those literature pieces which are thought-provoking in nature. During these days, when I sit alone in my room beside the window, while enjoying the fresh breeze of the jamrul tree beside my window I mostly read stories and poems of nature.

One day when I was reading 'The Book of Nature' by Ruskin Bond I could relate it so much with myself and my surroundings. The chapter named 'Trees' is my favorite because while reading the book and looking outside the window of my room, I can find a lot of similarities. It almost seems to me as if I am seeing the incidents of the books in front of my eyes. There in the chapter Bond talked about how ants build their nests with the leaves of trees. And I immediately looked at the 'Chico' plant or mud apple plant beside my window where ants have made their nest. Every day, I love to watch that how much laborious the ants are from morning to night. The most appreciable part of their whole effort is their effort and dedication in building that little nest. As they progresses daily, my level of amusement start rising and rising for I can't even believe that how skillful these little ants can be .I call these little red ants are master architects for they have mastered in the art of making such a beautiful tiny nest with just the leaves. Nature has so many wonders within it. And that's what Bond has also written in his book. And when I am seeing the same thing in front of my eyes, that's where literature and nature gets mingled.

One day, while I was reading Wordsworth's 'The Solitary Reaper' one of my all-time favorite poems of my favorite poet, there's line, 'A voice so thrilling never was heard/In the spring time from the cuckoo bird.' And I keep on relating to this one line again and again. For there are two or three cuckoos or probably more than that stay around my home and just with the advent of Spring ,they start singing at their fullest and sweetest from the crack of dawn to the shut of eve. Especially, in the spring mornings they come and sit in the boughs of the Jamrul tree just beside my window and start singing at their loudest. Their shrilling voice compels me to wake up at 4 o clock in the morning and look at the rising sun which almost looks like an egg yolk at that time. But I can best feel the thrilling quality of their voice which Wordsworth talked about during those moments of these house arrested days when I am not in a very happy mood. And I am honestly saying that their voices are truly thrilling for they can create magic in my mind. Whenever I hear their voices I temporarily forget all the negativities and my mind get filled with pleasure soon.

After these lockdown ,feel an oneness with nature.To me Nature became the only companion when I can't actually meet with my real companions with whom I spent times when everything was normal.And maybe because of being in such a solitary state I became more observant towards the nature.There's a fig tree in front of my balcony.A few months ago ,suddenly I saw that a couple of crested Bulbul birds were making their nest.The male bird used to gather straws and dried grasses and gradually made a beautiful nest.I felt almost baffled to see that these two little birds possess such a talent of making this compact nest which can save their younger ones from rain and heat.I love Bulbul birds for they sometimes come and sit on the grills of my window while their crests constantly move to and fro in the air.And whenever I see something amusing I call ma to share the amusement with her.There in the nights after dinner I and ma spend hours after hours talking about the amusing things which we see during daytime.Baba sometimes join us but most of the times I and ma talk so much that he have to become a silent listener.

To me rain or monsoon bears a lot of significance.Whenever rain starts I usually go to the balcony stand with my mother cuddling her.Ma always love watching rain.She hugs me and say, "Look at the sky ,see the clouds seems like dancing in the sky." I say her, "Remember ma ,when I was in class 2 ,you taught me a story named 'Meghomala' where the author said the clouds too have kings and princess within themselves." And thus our conversation regarding rain continues. Mostly in the rainy days I love to read poems which are based on rain.One afternoon as I was lying on my bed watching how the drops of water are trickling down the leaves of the plants placed outside my window suddenly I remember about the greatest Bengali poet Rabindranath Tagore for he has some of the fantastic songs and poems on monsoon.I started singing the song by him 'Aji jhoro jhoro mukhoro badal din e.'And as the rain increased while dark water filled clouds start coming from various directions to give us more rain ,it seemed in my eyes that from somewhere these monsoon clouds have got freedom and that's why they are rushing from the horizon towards the centre of the sky.And there's where Tagore's song again came to my mind, 'Ashar kotha hote aaj peli chara.' Tagore's poetry and creations are always relevant to our lives be it in the best of our times,be it in the most pensive hours of our lives.And specially this pandemic when our there are so much deaths,loses and wailings of sorrow in this atmosphere ,I have found Tagore in every moment of my life.I call Tagore's poetry as the best dictionary of all kinds of our emotions.

But one thing that I have learnt these days ,that literature can't be learned without discussions.The art of literary practice requires people around you who have an intense passion for literature.I am fortunate that I such literature loving people.Recently when Anisha ma'am completed teaching Shelley's 'Ode To The Wind wind' that very day ,in the evening the sky suddenly got overcastted and gradually a storm rose.It was a 'Kalbaishakhi jhor.'I opened the book kept it in front of my window and started reading the poem.The smell of the old book along with the smell of the rain created a different aura.And I could completely relate to Shelley's description of how the clouds gather from the horizon to the Zenith's height before bursting into rain.I told this to ma'am that I can see the actual scene of the storm in the same way Shelley described in the poem.Actually Anisha ma'am never keeps her teachings bound to the syllabus.She teaches us various genres of literature and sometimes I keep discussing with her about poems at length which are not even in our syllabus.And she says me that even though she teaches everything to us but poetry is her passion.And that's where the actual literature practice happens.Now whenever I read any new poems I immediately say that to her asking that , "Whether you have ever read it ma'am?" But to my utter surprise most of the times she says that, "Yes I have read this poem earlier." Everytime I try to give her a surprise by telling her to read some new poems expecting that she must have never even heard of this ,almost everytime I fail.For she has read poetry so extensively that most of the poems are known to her.Her omniscience in the field of poetry inspires me everytime.

Also during leisure times ,I and Oishee discuss about various literary works.If she reads something new she tells me to read that and if I read something new I tell her.During these pandemic she has completed reading so many books that I she herself also can't count the number.Mostly she talks about some of the best and exclusive books most of whose names I have never heard about.Whenever I write something new I send it to her and she critically analyzing it gives me the feedbacks which I love to listen.Literaure has been always there with us specially during the dark hours of pandemic.Starting from a literary debate to talking about modern literature ,I always get her beside me.Salwa sometimes join with us to enhance the literary discussions and thus we all combat with the pandemic by making literature our weapon.

# NOTE OF HOPE

There's a saying that 'After every darkness ,there is light.' And right at this moment we must remember this line for we are living through darkness.The pandemic outbreak has made us realize that we are just poor travelers between life and death.It has socially distanced us and have turned our everyday lives into a horror film.But inspite of all these ,we must have to carry on with our lives.It's our biggest challenge right now to save ourselves from mental illness.We have to accept the challenge of living and fighting with this pandemic instead of getting afraid of death.For every single moments when we can hear our heart beat its life.We have to find solace amidst all the darkness.

I personally feel that nature and good people around me who are helping me to survive in this tough time.Keeping our minds distracted in something is the most important thing during these days.I find peace in looking towards the nature.And there I find always something new everyday. We complain everyday and we do have reasons for complaining against this virus and the whole situation .But its actually useless.Rather we have to find out the best from the worst.Though this pandemic has brought innumerable troubles in our lives,but its because of this pandemic that people have got more time to spend with their families.Students like me,who had to run everytime have got time to share with my parents.And these moments of spending time with our parents will one day turn into memories.I'm spending the maximum time with my mother,trying to learn all her good qualities.Throughout the day ,my eyes followed her at every single moment. She is the sunshine of my life who is always there beside me everyday ,throughout the crests and troughs of daily life .Giving and finding time for ourselves and our hobbies are something that the pandemic has given us.We forgot amidst our hectic everyday schedules that who we are actually.I personally discovered a painter within myself.I never knew before that I have skills in painting for I never had time for myself . I never had time to think and explore the insight of myself.

And most importantly I would have never knew that I have such amazing people around me with whom my bond got more intensified when the pandemic separated us.The college became our dearest when we started longing to return back to that place.I terribly miss my college and sincerely wish to return back to our classrooms.When I went to my college in the month of February for some official works and library purposes ,I couldn't find that Heritage.Once our bustling college is now filled with an uncanny silent place ,where only birds and squirrels chirpings sounds can be heard.

But anyway,I think that if the nature can able to survive through all these furious cyclones and again reawakened with a new light of hope ,then why can't we.We will certainly overcome all the darkness and will soon see the disease-free, fearless dawntogether.

"We will rise up from the ashes and fire
We will survive through tears and fears
For we have power and hopes in our hearts
And will become victorious
For nothing is eternal ,not even ours sorrows and fears
They will soon get dried up by the new rays of the sun of hope and positivity."

www.ingramcontent.com/pod-product-compliance
Lightning Source LLC
LaVergne TN
LVHW050421160726
843469LV00041B/1182

* 9 7 8 9 3 5 4 5 8 5 3 6 4 *